The Beatles

Wise Publications
London/New York/Paris/Sydney/
Copenhagen/Madrid

Exclusive Distributors:
Music Sales Limited
8/9 Frith Street, London W1V 5TZ, England.
Music Sales Pty Limited
120 Rothschild Avenue, Rosebery, NSW 2018, Australia.

This book © Copyright 1994 by
Wise Publications
Order No. NO90571
ISBN 0-7119-3767-2

Cover design by Hutton Staniford
Compiled by Peter Evans
Music arranged by Stephen Duro
Music processed by Allegro Reproductions

Cover photograph Henry Grossman/REX

Music Sales' complete catalogue describes thousands of titles and is available in full colour sections by subject,
direct from Music Sales Limited. Please state your areas of interest and send a cheque/postal order for £1.50 for postage to:
Music Sales Limited, Newmarket Road, Bury St. Edmunds, Suffolk IP33 3YB.

Your Guarantee of Quality:
As publishers, we strive to produce every book to the highest commercial standards.

The music has been freshly engraved and the book has been carefully designed to minimise awkward page turns
and to make playing from it a real pleasure.

Particular care has been given to specifying acid-free, neutral-sized paper made from pulps which have not been
elemental chlorine bleached. This pulp is from farmed sustainable forests and was produced with special regard for
the environment. Throughout, the printing and binding have been planned to ensure a sturdy, attractive publication
which should give years of enjoyment.

If your copy fails to meet our high standards, please inform us and we will gladly replace it.

Printed in the United Kingdom

Blackbird

Words & Music by John Lennon & Paul McCartney

All You Need Is Love

Words & Music by John Lennon & Paul McCartney

Moderately

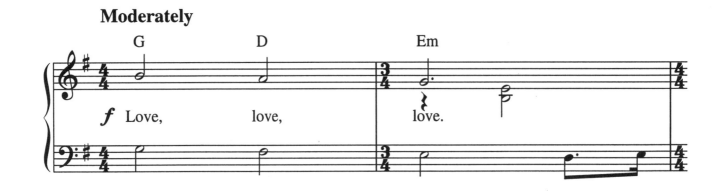

Love,   love,   love.

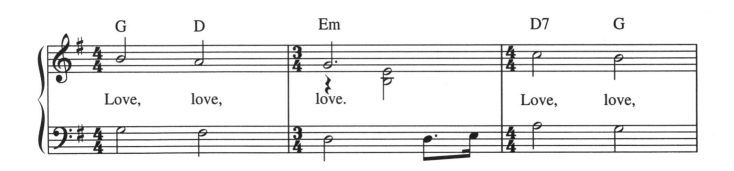

Love,   love,   love.   Love,   love,

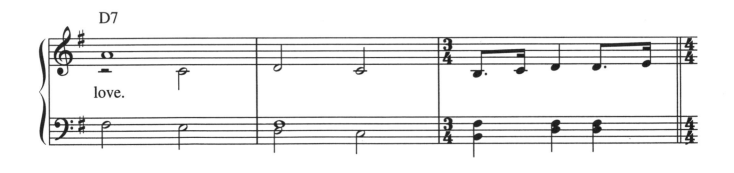

love.

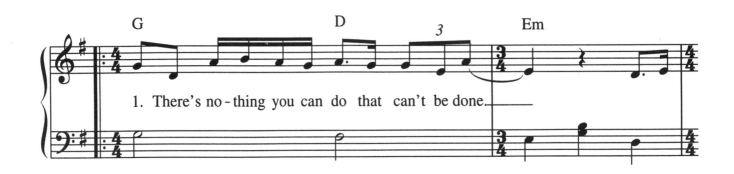

1. There's no-thing you can do that can't be done.

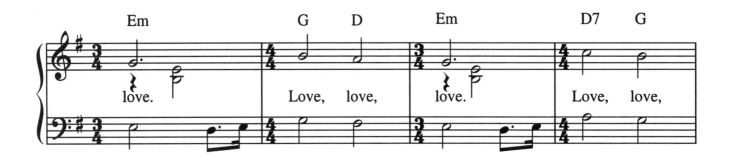

2. There's nothing you can make that can't be made,
   No one you can save that can't be saved.
   Nothing you can do but you can learn how to be you in time.
   It's easy.

3. There's nothing you can know that isn't known.
   Nothing you can see that isn't shown.
   Nowhere you can be that isn't where you're meant to be.
   It's easy.

Day Tripper

Words & Music by John Lennon & Paul McCartney

Moderate rock

1. Got a good rea - son for tak - ing the eas - y way out.

Got a good rea - son_____ for

tak - ing the eas - y way out___ now. She was a day_____

2. She's a big teaser,
   She took me half the way there.
   She's a big teaser,
   She took me half the way there, now.
   She was a day tripper,
   One way ticket, yeah!
   It took me so long to find out
   And I found out.

3. Tried to please her,
   She only played one night stands.
   Tried to please her,
   She only played one night stands, now.
   She was a day tripper,
   Sunday driver, yeah!
   It took me so long to find out
   And I found out.

Dear Prudence

Words & Music by John Lennon & Paul McCartney

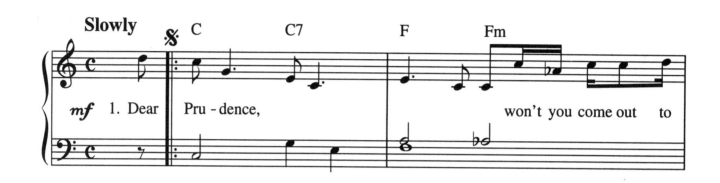

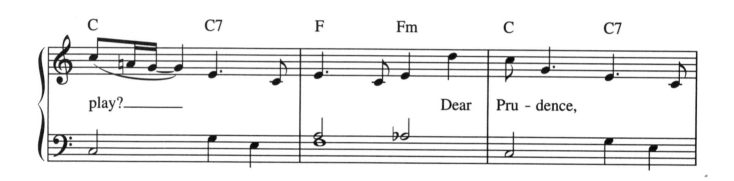

2. Dear Prudence, open up your eyes,
   Dear Prudence, see the sunny skies.
   The wind is low, the birds will sing that you are
     part of ev'rything,
   Dear Prudence, won't you open up your eyes?
   Look around, *(etc.)*

3. Dear Prudence, let me see you smile,
   Dear Prudence, like a little child.
   The clouds will be a daisy chain so let me
     see you smile again,
   Dear Prudence, won't you let me see you smile?
   Look around, *(etc.)*

4. *Verse 4 as Verse 1*

Do You Want To Know A Secret?

Words & Music by John Lennon & Paul McCartney

Freely

Moderately

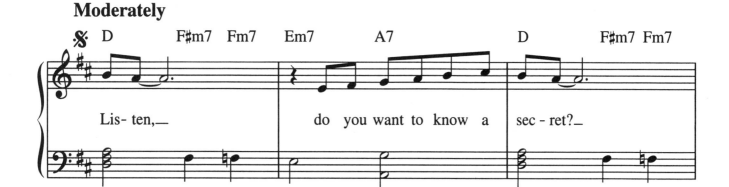

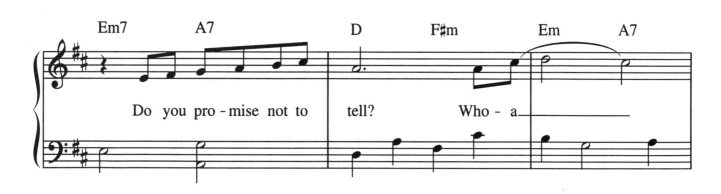

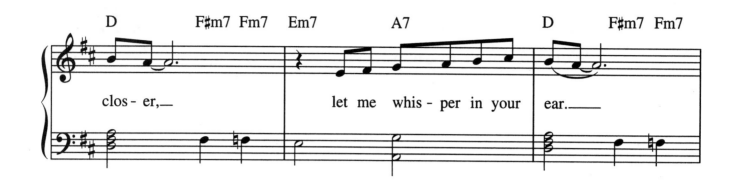

clos - er,—   let me whis - per in your ear.—

Say   the   words   I   love   to   hear,————————

— I'm— in love with   you.———   Oo,—————

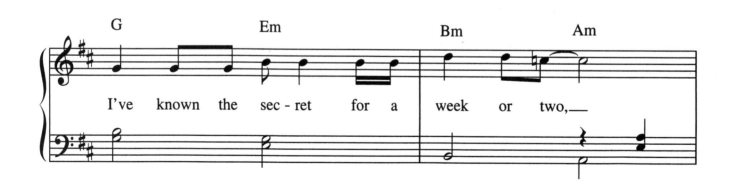

I've   known   the   sec - ret   for   a   week   or   two,—

No - bo - dy knows, just we two.

D.S. al Coda

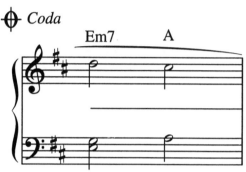

Coda

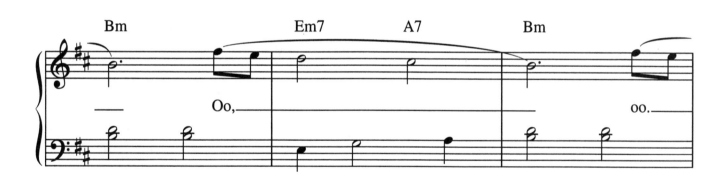

Oo,_____ oo.

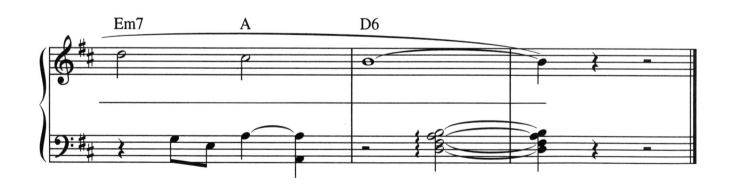

Hello Goodbye

Words & Music by John Lennon & Paul McCartney

Help!

Words & Music by John Lennon & Paul McCartney

Moderately

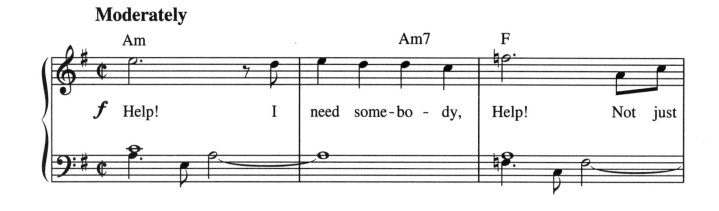

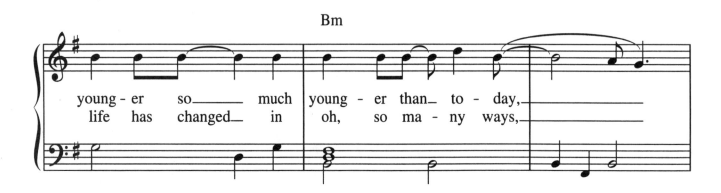

Here, There And Everywhere

Words & Music by John Lennon & Paul McCartney

I Feel Fine

Words & Music by John Lennon & Paul McCartney

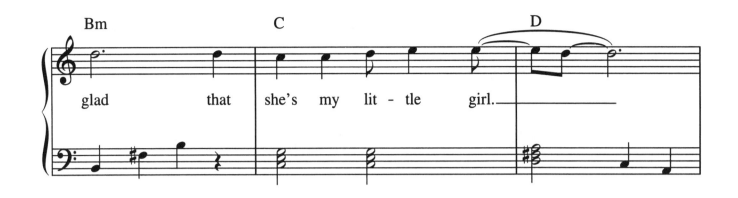

glad   that   she's   my   lit - tle   girl.

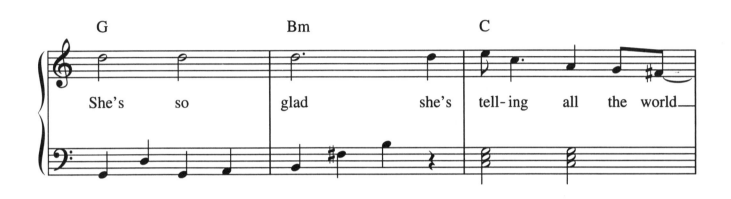

She's   so   glad   she's   tell-ing   all   the   world

That   her   ba - by   buys   her   things   you know,   he

buys   her   dia - mond rings   you know,   she   said   so.

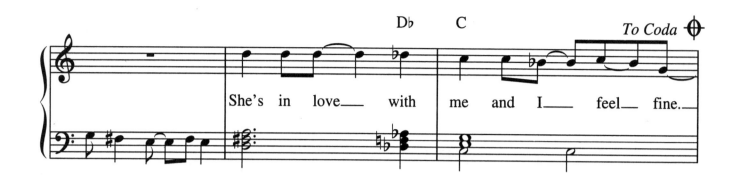

She's in love___ with me and I___ feel__ fine.__

She's in love__ with me and I____ feel__ fine.__

Please Please Me

Words & Music by John Lennon & Paul McCartney

Moderately

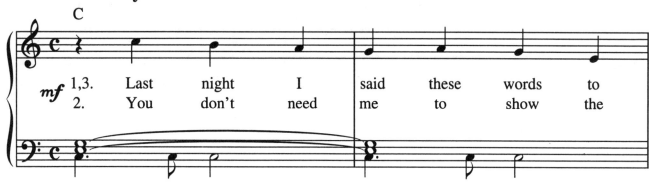

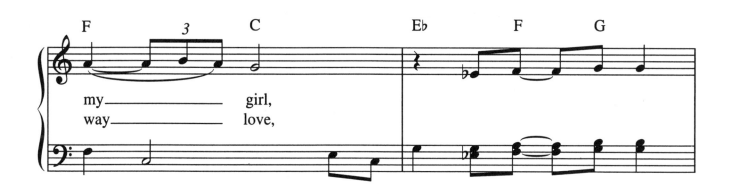

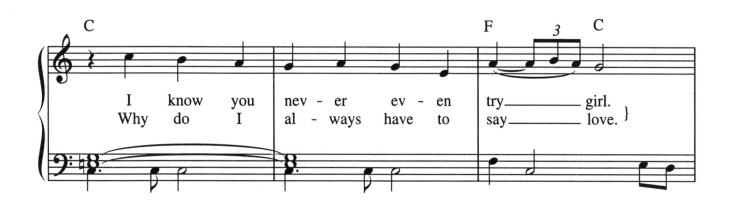

on, (come on)___ Come on, (come on)___ Please please me, oh

yeah, like I please you.

I don't want to sound com - plain - ing

but you know there's al - ways rain in my___ heart,

(in my heart). I do all the pleas - ing with you,

It's so hard to rea - son with you, oh yeah, Why do you make me

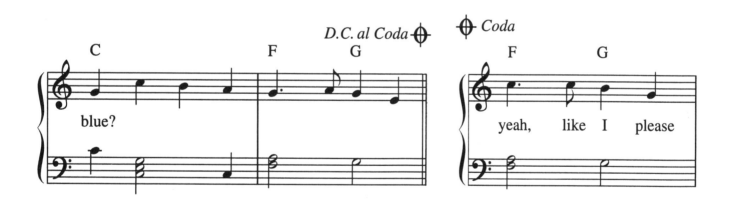

D.C. al Coda ⊕⎯ ⊕ *Coda*

blue? yeah, like I please

you, oh yeah, like I please you._____

Nowhere Man

Words & Music by John Lennon & Paul McCartney

Revolution

Words & Music by John Lennon & Paul McCartney

Moderate shuffle

f 1. You say you want a re - vo - lu - tion_____ well,_____ you know,_____

we all want to change the world.

You tell me that it's ev - o - lu - tion_____ well_____

_____ you know,_____ we all want to change the

world. ____

But when you talk a - bout de-

struc - tion, _____

Don't you know that you can count me out. _

Don't you know it's gon - na be al -

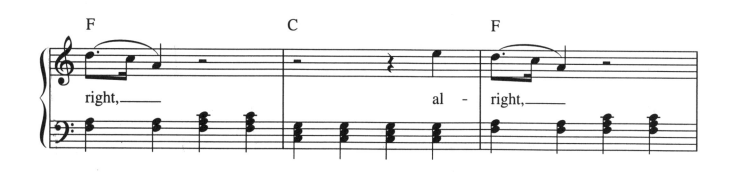

right, _____

al - right, _____

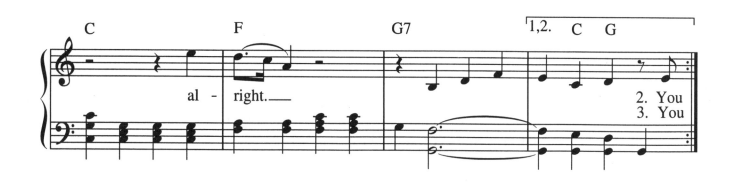

al - right. ___

2. You
3. You

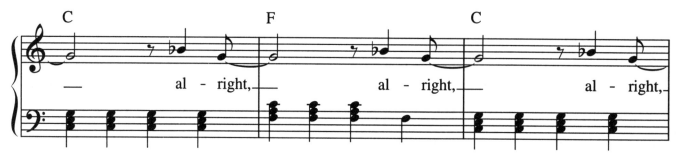

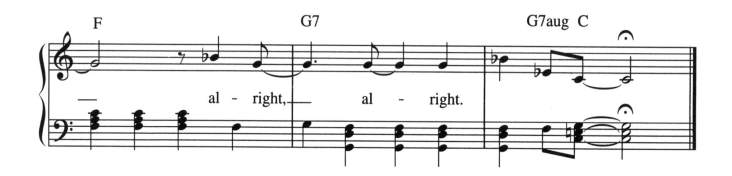

2. You say you got a real solution,
   Well you know,
   We'd all love to see the plan.
   You ask me for a contribution,
   Well you know,
   We're all doing what we can.
   But if you want money for people with minds that hate,
   All I can tell you is "Brother you have to wait."
   Don't you know it's gonna be alright.

3. You say you'll change the constitution,
   Well you know,
   We all want to change your head.
   You tell me it's the institution,
   Well you know,
   You better free your mind instead.
   But if you go carrying pictures of Chairman Mao,
   You ain't going to make it with anyone anyhow.
   Don't you know it's gonna be alright.

She's Leaving Home

Words & Music by John Lennon & Paul McCartney

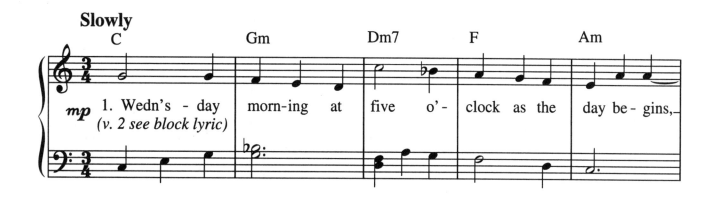

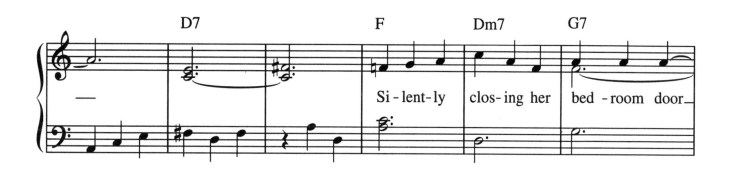

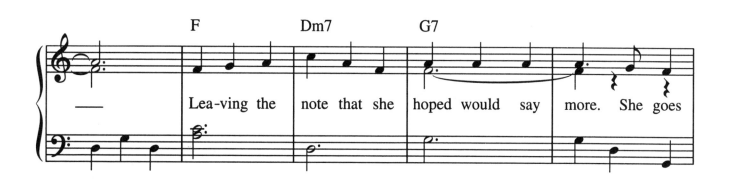

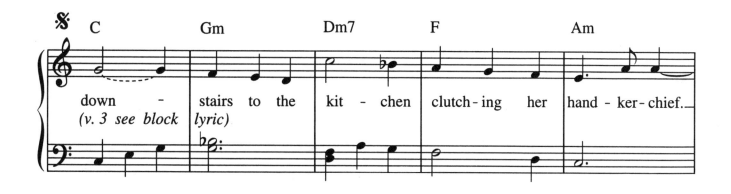

38

2. Father snores as his wife gets into her dressing gown,
   Picks up the letter that's lying there.
   Standing alone at the top of the stairs,
   She breaks down and cries to her husband
   "Daddy, our baby's gone."
   Why would she treat us so thoughtlessly
   How could she do this to me?
   She (we never thought of ourselves) is leaving
   (Never a thought of ourselves)
   Home (we struggled hard all our lives to get by).

3. Friday morning at nine o'clock she is far away.
   Waiting to keep the appointment she made.
   Meeting a man from the motor trade.
   She (what did we do that was wrong) is leaving
   (We didn't know it was wrong)
   Home (fun is the one thing that money can't buy).
   Something inside that was always denied for so many years.

Strawberry Fields Forever

Words & Music by John Lennon & Paul McCartney

Slowly

Let me take you down 'cause I'm go-in' to Straw-ber-ry

Fields. Noth-ing is real, and noth-ing to get hung a-bout;

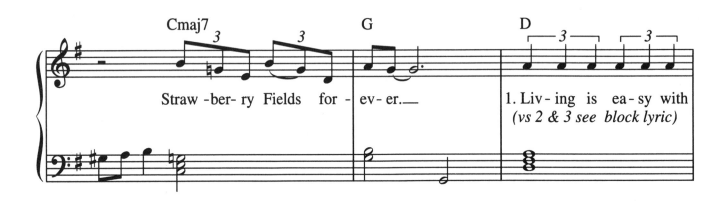

Straw-ber-ry Fields for-ev-er.__ 1. Liv-ing is ea-sy with *(vs 2 & 3 see block lyric)*

eyes closed, mis-un-der-stand-ing all you see.__

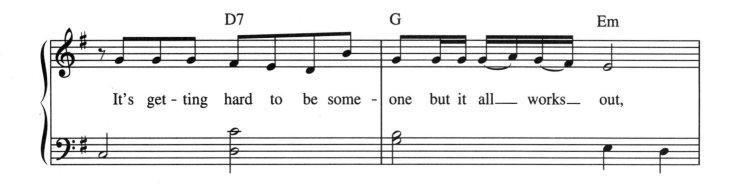

It's get-ting hard to be some - one but it all— works— out,

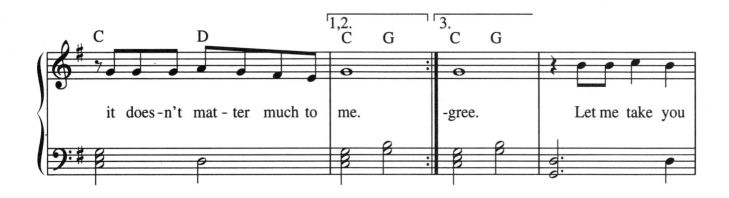

it does-n't mat-ter much to me. -gree. Let me take you

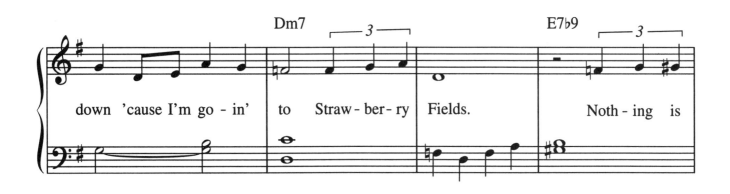

down 'cause I'm go - in' to Straw - ber - ry Fields. Noth - ing is

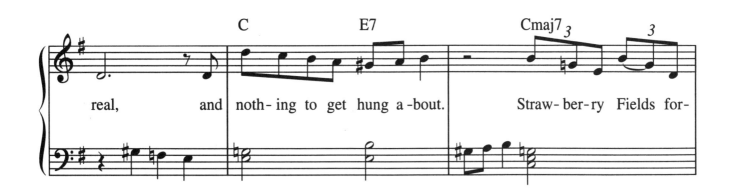

real, and noth-ing to get hung a-bout. Straw-ber-ry Fields for-

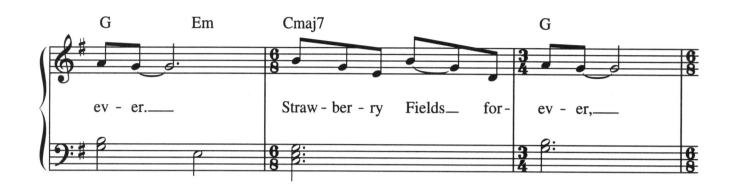

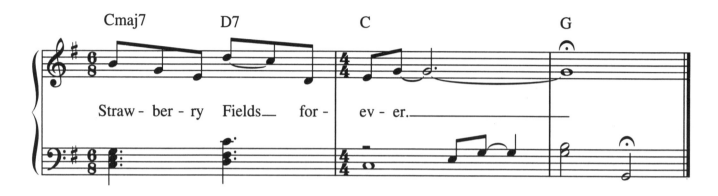

2. No one I think is in my tree,
   I mean it must be high or low.
   That is you know you can't tune in,
   But it's all right.
   That is I think it's not too bad.
   Let me take you down *(etc.)*.

3. Always, no sometimes, think it's me,
   But you know I know when it's a dream.
   I think I know of thee, ah yes,
   But it's all wrong,
   That is I think I disagree.
   Let me take you down *(etc.)*.

The Long And Winding Road

Words & Music by John Lennon & Paul McCartney

Slowly

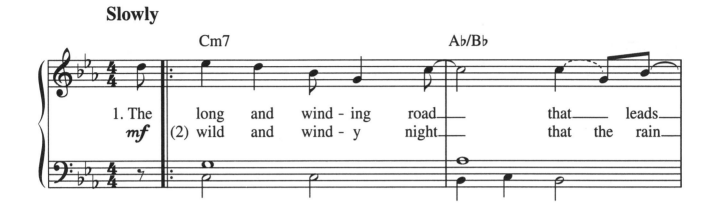

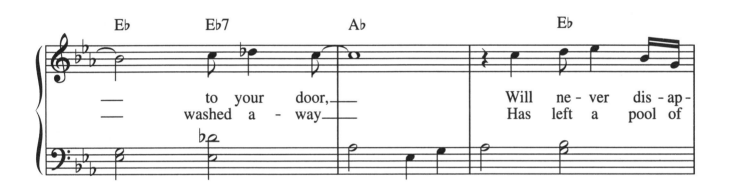

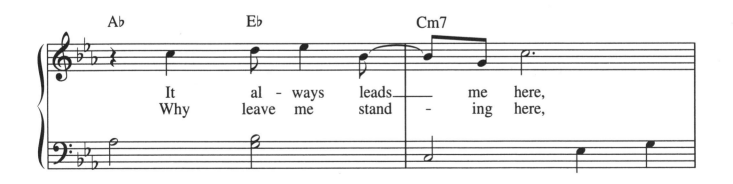

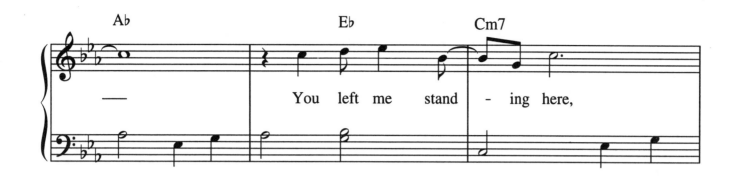

You left me stand - ing here,

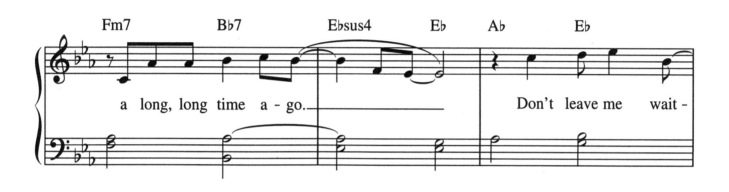

a long, long time a - go. Don't leave me wait -

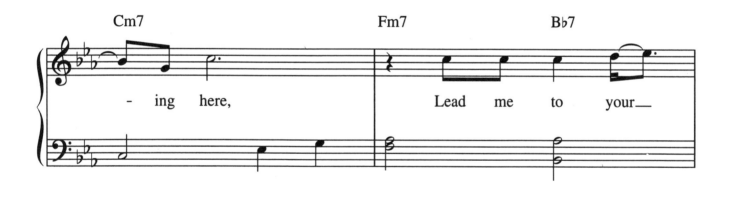

- ing here, Lead me to your

door. Yeah, yeah, yeah, yeah.

We Can Work It Out

Words & Music by John Lennon & Paul McCartney

Moderately slow

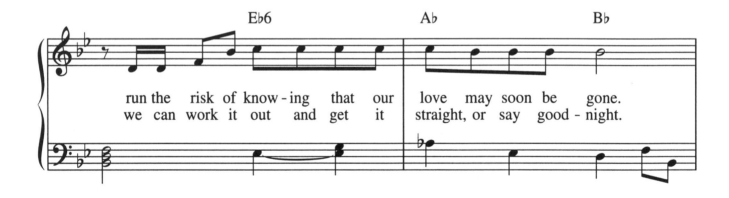

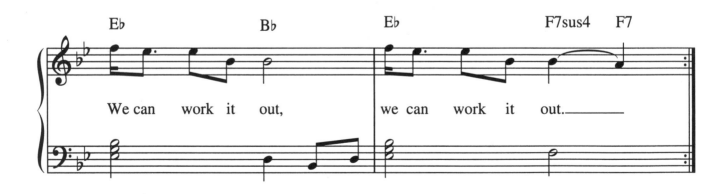

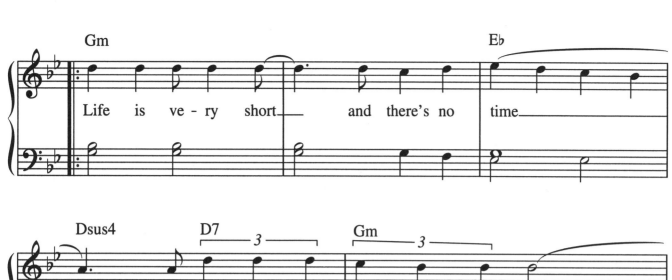

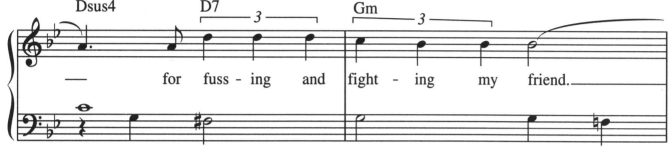

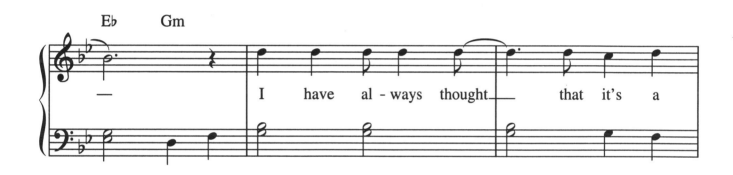

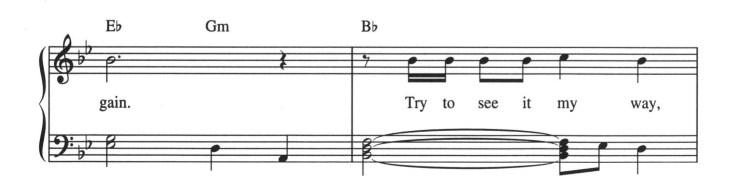

on - ly time will tell if I am right or I am wrong.

While you see it your way, there's a chance that we might fall a-

part be - fore too long. We can work it out,

we can work it out.____

11/02 (45970)